INTROVERTS

HOW TO USE YOUR HIDDEN STRENGTHS TO SUCCEED IN AN EXTROVERT WORLD

Table of Contents

Introduction

This book contains proven steps and strategies on how to lead a successful social, professional and personal life despite being an introvert in an 'extrovert-ideal' world. Societal perceptions of intelligence, competence, and intellectual ability are usually associated with extroversion, which makes the life of an introvert all the more challenging.

Before anything else, you need to understand that there is nothing wrong with being an introvert. The day you start believing this fact will be the day you will start to appreciate your own potential. History has it that the most brilliant minds of the world were introverts. However, if you live in the 'extrovert-ideal' world, all you will receive is taunts and remarks. You need to turn these into opportunities to prove that there is nothing wrong in being a thinker and innovator. It is fine if you like to spend time alone, thinking about the more important things in life rather than partying all night long in the pub.

While accepting your personality and living with it is one aspect of the story, you will also need to fine-tune your personality to bring the best out of you and beat the 'extrovert-ideal' world at their own game. You will need to change your mindset to network with people and become more social. Humans are social animals and until and unless you network with people, you cannot achieve much in the modern world. Introverts don't like to socialize with strangers, but this does not mean that they don't like to socialize at all. As an introvert, you need to work on these skills to gain a better position.

What is an Introvert?

Human personality is a complex combination of several traits. One of the most common and significant personality trait identified by many diverse theories is introversion. As the word and its meaning suggest, introversion is a personality trait in which the individual tends to turn inwards and pays heed to him or her *own self's* internal feeling and thoughts. In other words, such people do not require an external stimulation to think, focus or work on.

Introversion is a parallel and opposite concept for extraversion. While extraversion forms one end of the scale, introversion lies on the other extreme end. Several theories have mentioned and emphasized the importance of both these personality traits, introversion, and extraversion. In fact, a few theories have also indicated that every individual has a degree of both these traits. However, the inclination of the individual towards one end or the other largely depends on the intensity of these traits.

Owing to the inward-looking personality of introverts, these people usually tend to be reserved, quiet and introspective. Extroverts require external stimuli and get their energy from social interactions. On the contrary, introverts spend their energy whenever they are forced into a social interaction so much so that post a gathering, introverts prefer to remain alone to recharge their spent energies.

Introversion and shyness are two different terms that are commonly used interchangeably. However, there is a fine line that exists between these two personality traits. While introversion is a liking of the quiet and lonely, shyness is a condition where the individual fears being judged negatively. A popular theory in this area maps introversion/extroversion on one axis and calm/anxious on the other axis. As a result of this classification, four quadrants namely, calm/anxious extroverts and calm/anxious introverts come into existence.

Despite being evidently differently, introversion and shyness are usually considered as related. There are several reasons for such a linkage. Firstly, the society has a clear bias against both these personality traits. Although, the mental state of an extrovert who is shy at the moment and is not speaking is not the same as an introvert who is just in a calm state of mind. While the former fears speaking, the latter isn't just interested in the outside world as he or she is over stimulated by the world inside. The one common thing between these two personality traits is that both of them are disliked by the society. It is a general perception to like people who are talkative and open. They are just considered more competent and smart than their counterparts.

With this said, a little overlap between shyness and introversion also exists. Although the degree is uncertain, most people who are shy are usually introverts and introversion may also lead to shyness in a lot of cases. There can be a lot of reasons behind this. Introverts are time and time again told that there is something wrong with them. This may cause them to fear social interactions, leading to shyness. On the other hand, shyness may compel people to explore the world of solitude, which is what introversion is. Besides this, some people are just born with these two traits in their personality.

Evidently, there lies a mild overlap between shyness and introversion. However, the overlap is not so much that these terms can be used interchangeably. Moreover, the treatment that people get from society when they are assumed to be shy when they are actually introverts and vice-versa is maddening. Imagine, how awkward would it be for an introvert engrossed in his or her thinking world to be instructed by a stranger to smile as if he or she is fighting depression.

Lastly, both shyness and introversion are associated with submissiveness, which, in the competitive world, is not a good trait to possess. This is perhaps the reason why both these personality traits are looked down upon by society. They are just not perceived as smart, good and competent. As a result, most introverts and shy people lead a life of loneliness, spending their time studying or inventing something the world hasn't yet thought about. So, they may not be able to play active roles in society, but their passive presence creates role models like no other.

Types of Introverts

We've already established the complexity of the introvert personality in the previous chapters. You might be wondering by now why some of the basic signs of being an introvert apply to you while some do not. Does that mean you are not an introvert? Or perhaps, you are a semi-introvert or maybe, you're just someone who has a tendency to change from being an introvert to an extrovert? Worry not because the truth is, being an introvert is too complex to just label someone as being one. You do not have to possess all the characteristics associated with introversion to be a complete introvert.

According to Jonathan Cheek, a professor of personality psychology, introverts can be further categorized into four types. Social introverts, thinking introverts, anxious introverts and restrained introverts. They can easily be remembered by using the acronym, *STAR*. If you have a strong feeling that you are an introvert but you are somehow holding back because you do not possess all the characteristics, here are the different types of introverts, explained.

Try to identify which one you belong to by honestly answering the corresponding questions after each type.

Social Introverts

Social introversion covers a majority of the common traits people normally identify with introverts. It is the preference for a smaller social group rather than a large one. Social introverts identify few people as their close friends and tend to only socialize with them. It does not have to be a group, though. Social introverts are also fine with enjoying the company of two people, or the company of one best friend, or having no company at all.

Questions to ask yourself:

Do you prefer celebrating occasions with a few friends rather than a bunch of people?

Do you have a close relationship with your friends?

Do you see being around other people not necessary most of the time?

Do you prefer doing things alone?

Do you not say much about yourself?

Do you feel drained during social celebrations despite the fact that you enjoyed yourself?

If you answered yes to all these questions, you are definitely a social introvert.

Thinking Introverts

Social events are not a problem to thinking introverts although they still possess dominant qualities introverts are known to have. They are introspective, self-reflective, insightful and imaginative. These introverts have great control over their thinking. Professor Cheek even said that they are capable of creating a fantasy world in their mind through their imagination, a clear sign of creativity and cleverness.

Questions to ask yourself:

Do you regularly assess your thoughts and ideas about yourself?

Do you imagine yourself being in the same situation as the character whenever you watch movies or read books?

Do you always pay attention to what you feel?

Do you value your own evaluation about yourself?

Do you sometimes, daydream and fantasize about your future?

If you answered yes to all these questions, you are a certified thinking introvert.

Anxious Introverts

Unlike other introverts who seek solitude to recharge, anxious introverts seek it to escape social situations. They easily feel awkward at social interactions and are not quite confident about themselves. They are the type of introverts who get anxious about several things. They have tendencies to remember all the awkwardness and embarrassing moments that happened throughout the day before going to sleep. Although being alone does not make the anxiety fade away, it helps these introverts cope with their current situation and analyze the positive things they can do next. It also recharges their energy just like it does to other introverts.

Questions to ask yourself:

Do you often feel like everyone is looking at you?

Do you often think about the bad memories of your past?

Do you get ashamed or angry about defeat?

Do you still feel alone even when you are in a group of friends?

Do you find it hard to overcome your shyness in new situations?

If you answered yes to all these questions, most probably, you are an anxious introvert.

Restrained Introverts

This type of introversion is the perfect example of what a reserved person is. They tend to be silent most of the time and they always process their thoughts before speaking or taking action. Another thing that distinguishes restrained introverts from other types of introverts is their slow pace. They do not engage in activities as soon as they wake up. They usually think about things and assess probable consequences before they perform an action. A restrained introvert tends to start their day a little late and is generally not a morning person.

Questions to ask yourself:

Do you find it hard to be off and running as soon as you wake up in the morning?

Do you take things slow and easy in order for you to relax?

Do you process your thoughts slowly before speaking?

Do you often feel the need to scrutinize the situation first before taking any action?

Do you often feel sluggish?

If you answered yes to all these questions then consider yourself as a restrained introvert.

Famous Introverts

Albert Einstein and Sir Isaac Newton, two of the most important contributors in the field of science, were actually introverts. In politics, you have the former president of the United States, Barack Obama who was also the first African-American president in the US. Hillary Clinton, a former first lady of US, is also an introvert. Mark Zuckerberg who is the founder and current CEO of one of the most famous social networking site, and Bill Gates, the philanthropist who founded Microsoft, are both introverts who have made a huge impact on today's modern society.

The famous Michael Jordan is one of the greatest introvert athletes who have inspired many basketball players. The creator of the Wizarding World of Harry Potter, JK Rowling is also an introvert, herself.

There are even celebrities who happen to be introverts as well. To name a few, there is Emma Watson, Johnny Depp, Lady Gaga, Christina Aguilera, Audrey Hepburn and Zayn Malik. Imagine the courage all of them had to take to get used to cameras and paparazzi.

<u>What Are the Strengths of an Introvert?</u>

Now that you understand your personality's weaknesses, the next thing you would want to act on is your boundless set of strengths. Introverts do have some idea about what their talents and capabilities are, but they cannot yet create a whole picture of with it. They cannot be certain in themselves of these potentials because they have little to no actual experience of putting it to the test. So, to help you with this, here are a few known strengths that most introverts would have.

Independence

Independence is one of your innate characteristics so do not take it for granted. Utilize it because not everyone is capable of doing things alone. With it, you are also more confident, fearing less things and be ready to conquer whatever the future may bring. Remember that your life is mostly made up of your own decisions. You are the captain of your own ship. You decide which path you walk, which way you go. Nobody can tell you what to do.

You can be trusted with any job or task. In school, your teachers probably do not have to oversee you. You can discipline yourself. In the workplace, your boss would not have to regularly remind you of your deadlines. You are also less likely to be in conflict with your supervisors. Upper-level officers believe that you can produce quality output on time.

Self-trust

One of the greatest things that independence can develop in people is self-trust. Self-trust is vital towards your ability to stay firm amid the rapid changes in your surroundings. With it, you are not susceptible to any malicious influence. People will find it hard to negatively influence you. Your solid stand on things is not easy to destroy. You believe that you are accountable for everything that happens to your life. You are able to learn from your own shortcomings and believe that you can stand up every time you fall down.

Leadership

When you combine independence and self-trust, you have some of the most essential qualities that a good leader must have. At its very core, the idea of leadership is being able to work with your members equally in order for the team to function as one. As an introvert, you have the unique ability to read what your team's strengths and weaknesses are—in doing so, you would be able to delegate tasks intelligently. Since you're also a great listener, you would be able to sympathize with their needs quite easily. Observational skills provide you with the ability to give advice that no one else might have thought of. Simple things, really, but they make all the difference.

A Great Artist

For the most part, many introverts are actually a bit more artistically inclined when compared to others. They tend to see things differently; sometimes, in a deeper and more thoughtful manner. As they are not always the best when it comes to vocalizing these things, many introverted people turn to art as a medium for expression. Painting, sketching, music, theater and even writing are just a few of the most common choices for them.

It's all about finding what you're most comfortable with and developing what you're most passionate about.

Effective Communication Skill

This may seem surprising but many introverts actually possess the potential of being a good speaker and this is due to certain characteristics they inherently possess.

Being a good listener is one of those characteristics. If you are used to listening to people then you are aware of the subjects that compel them to really pay attention. You are more capable of adjusting the formality, tone, and level of words you need to use in order to get your point across.

If good speakers catch their audience's attention with their words, the best speakers catch attention with their wit. Think of this as an opportunity to stretch your creative muscles and create speeches based on your observation of people. Remember that one way of connecting effectively with people is by finding common ground with them; as an introvert, this is also among your many talents, the ability to sympathize with whoever you may be conversing with.

Proper Judgment

It should be clear to you by now that your ultimate weapon is your mind. It could go places even if your body, physically could not. One thing it does is collectively process data and form judgments. If you are an introvert, it is not easy for you to hastily settle on a final decision. Unlike extroverts who usually judge objectively, you regard information subjectively.

You don't just use evidence to rush into conclusions. You use other factors to help you analyze situations carefully such as external forces or abnormalities in the environment. You believe solving a case is not just for the sake of settling things in the present but it can also be used to derive solutions for the future. Your way of judging can both be disadvantageous and advantageous. Always use your critical thinking when finalizing decisions.

How Can an Introvert Use Their Strengths to Succeed?

The world is not a stage where the audience can only see the performers. It is an entire production, a whole crew that puts everything together. Each one puts in an equal amount of effort in order to create the best production possible. In the same manner, the world is not only composed of extroverts, the people who would often appear on stage. The crew is also comprised of introverts who help keep things running even while they stay back from the limelight. After all, most introverts are happier simply doing their thing in the backstage.

So, what rules would apply to introverts in our society?

Here are a few examples:

Provides Balance

Where there are storytellers, there would also be listeners. Introverts provide a much-needed balance by simply being themselves. Introverts are everywhere in our society and wherever they might be placed, they bring their strengths along with them. These are the people who observe quietly and apply what they have learned accordingly; the people with a keen eye for detail, who highlight the things we may have missed. Without them, the balance of energies between people will not exist and we can argue that society may not even function as it should.

Can you imagine a world where there are only extroverted people?

A New Way of Looking at Things

As established earlier, introverts tend to have a deeper perspective on the things that happen around them. The society benefits in many ways from this, especially when it comes to finding solutions for problems that might seem challenging at first. To find the best answer to a riddle, two differing opinions need to be considered; the common answer and the other that's a little out of the box.

Without people who are capable of creative thought, can there really be any progress? This is one of the reasons why people with unique perspectives are important to the whole.

<u>Friendships</u>

It is not natural for an introvert to go out and socialize with people. However, this doesn't mean that introverts don't like to spend time with their friends. They love to have good friends and share a good bonding with them. With that said, the most difficult part of a friendship or relationship for an introvert is to approach people and be more social. This will also mean that they will have to come out of their comfort zone and work against their natural instincts. This chapter discusses ways and methods that you can use to alter your introversion for a better social life and making it easier for you to leave your comfort zone to meet new people.

Learn About Friendship Preferences

Every human has a different way of making friends. While some people like to make only close and dear friends, others may be fine with casual friendships. There is another class of people who are not interested in making any close friends. They just like to confide in their family. It is important to understand the friendship preferences of people.

If you are looking for close friendships, you need to realize that establishing and maintaining such relationships are not going to be easy. Therefore, before you plan any such thing, give yourself some time to ask yourself if the person has the time and commitment that you are looking for in a friend. It is impossible to make friends with a person unless you have compatible friendship preferences. Remember this as a rule!

Use Social Rituals

Understandably, your natural instincts will not help you become more social. Therefore, you will need to look for ways and means that can compel you to socialize. One of the best ways you can do this is by setting conditions so you won't have to think a lot about socializing and just do it. Social rituals can be instrumental in helping you make this possible. For instance, you can set aside an hour from your schedule and make it a point to connect with people you know in this time. Besides this, you must also create a monthly social schedule. This will be a time frame set aside for you to meet new people and make new contacts.

These schedules can be simple reminders in your phone to catch up with old friends on a weekly basis and network with new people on a monthly basis. This can be the first thing you do at the beginning of the week so that you can spend the rest of the week believing that you are socializing enough and not ignoring people. You can materialize these schedules in a better way by taking a club membership. You should be committed to visit this club every week and attend monthly events that they organize to help you meet new people. Make it a point to choose one club and stay with it. If you still believe that you will find ways to escape the events, you can choose to join the organizing committee for events. In this way, you won't have an option. You will have to attend all the functions no matter what. These social rituals will help you monitor and control your social life.

Let Your Social Life Work on Its Own

The amount of effort required in creating a social circle will radically reduce if you change the way you think about friendship and how you hope to move ahead with them. Most importantly, you need to shift your focus from individual friends to groups of friends. You might have many individual friends and it is always a good idea to help these friends connect with each other. Start with introducing them to each other. This is the first step towards forming groups of friends.

Although this may seem like a small thing at first, you will be surprised by the kind of effect it can have on your general social life. When your friends know each other and form a group, they will keep on planning something or the other. As a result, you will not be required to plan to connect with your friends. Someone somewhere will always have a meet-up and catch-up plan ready for you. In this manner, your existing social circle will become self-managed and you can now concentrate on creating new social circles.

Leave Your Comfort Zone

The commonest remark you must have got from people, as an introvert, is 'get out of your shell'. The society isn't happy with the idea of an introvert being comfortable in his or her loneliness. Such advice may be annoying and may even force a person to do exactly the opposite of what they are expected to do. This is all the more true for introverts. They tend to retract back into their shells whenever they are asked to alter their behavior.

So, what is this shell? Introverts are like turtles. They carry a shell with themselves everywhere they go. Social situations are a perfect example of where you can see how the shell works. Most introverts take a friend along with them to parties to avoid unfavorable circumstances. It is noteworthy at this stage to mention that the shell we are talking about is different for each individual. Take the example of an individual who is expected to sing on the stage in front of a panel of judges. However, the person has experience in performing on stage, but not for singing. The person is sure to be uncomfortable while performing in front of the judges, but viewing it from the perspective that he stands a better chance and is perhaps lesser uncomfortable than a person who has no stage experience. This is a perfect example of how people stretch their comfort zone and expand it based on their past experiences.

Looking beyond the comfort zone and expanding it will require a shift in mindset. You will need to look at things differently. For instance, if you look at a dinner date as a lifetime, life-changing experience, you are sure to get overwhelmed. However, if you see it as an experiment, handling the situation will be all that *easier*. All in all, you don't really need to move out of your comfort zone.

All you need to do is expand your comfort zone to a point that can help adjust to your surroundings.

Dating

In the previous chapters, we discussed how interesting and amazing an introvert can be and you need to know these things if you are going to prepare yourself for dating. If you want to be successful at dating, you have to know your value or you will end up dating those who are only going to take advantage of you and your dating life will not be successful at all.

We all know that it is difficult for introverts to be around large groups of people and many introverts feel that this could cause them to lose out when it comes to finding love. They also think that since they like to spend their free time alone that they cannot have a successful relationship.

As an introvert, you may feel like everyone that is of the opposite sex is looking for a partner with an extrovert type of personality. You need to understand that it does not matter if you are an extrovert or an introvert when it comes to dating. What does matter is that you have the tools that are needed to ensure that you are successful at dating and that is what I am going to give you in this book.

One of the things that you have to do before you can be successful at dating is to prepare yourself for dating. Of course, that is one of the reasons that you are reading this book, but it goes much deeper than that. If you want to prepare yourself for dating, whether you are an introvert or an extrovert, the first thing you need to do is start with yourself.

You need to ensure that you have a life that is not only interesting but that you enjoy. You will need to have things to talk about and if you are a boring person then chances are that you will bore your date. You should also realize that if you are not happy with your life and happy with yourself, you will not be happy with someone else.

Dating and being in a relationship is not about filling some void within yourself, you need to do that long before you begin dating. This means that if you are dating in order to fill some type of void you need to take a step back and take a good look at your life.

There are several adjustments that you can make in order to fill that void. You should make sure that you enjoy your job. If you are working in an area that you do not enjoy you will find that you complain about your job a lot. People are attracted to those who love what they do for a living and love talking about it instead of complaining about it. You should also consider finding a hobby that you enjoy. Of course, if you are an introvert, this hobby may be something that you can quietly do alone and that is completely fine as long as it brings you some joy.

The point is that you should remove as much of the negativity from your life as you can and do things that you enjoy. People want to date happy people, not people who are miserable and complain all of the time.

The second thing that you need to do in order to prepare yourself for dating is to figure out where you can begin meeting people. Since you are not the type of person who is going to be found sitting at a bar or hanging out at a club, you need to look at the areas you frequent and decide which places would be appropriate to start meeting people.

One thing that many introverts find is that they prefer to start online. The idea is not that you are going to find the love of your life online, but that you are going to learn how to better interact with people and open up to them. You will also begin to understand what people are looking for in a partner.

Online dating is great for introverts because it allows you to take time and think about what you are going to say before you say it. The downside is that if you are like most introverts you loathe being messaged all of the time and this happens quite often when you are part of an online dating community. This means that a lot of messages go unanswered and feelings get hurt.

Some people will tell you that work is a great place to look for a date and although I do feel that socializing a bit at work is okay and will help you learn how to better interact with others I do not suggest dating anyone from your job. You need to keep your work and your social life separate as much as possible.

Think about other places that you frequent, possibly church, school, the grocery store or even a coffee shop. All of these places are great places for you to think about when you are trying to determine places where you could possibly meet a potential partner.

Flirting For an Introvert

Now that you know where you can meet someone you need to understand how you can flirt with that person. As an introvert, flirting does not come naturally like it does for an extrovert so this is something that you will have to learn.

Learning how to flirt will also help you when it comes to understanding if someone is flirting with you. One of the biggest issues with being an introvert when it comes to dating is confusing someone who is flirting with someone who is just being nice.

One of the best ways that you can flirt with someone that you are attracted to is to simply be polite. This is one of the main reasons why so many people confuse someone who is polite with someone that is flirting. It is because being polite is actually seen as a form of flirting. Of course, being polite alone is not enough because as you already know not everyone who is polite is flirting so you will need to add in a few more elements.

Make sure that you pay attention to what the other person is saying and how they are acting. This will allow you to understand how they are really feeling and will make them feel important to you.

Another way for introverts to flirt is to be playful. This is one of the easiest ways to flirt. Instead of forcing yourself to be serious and putting deep thought into your every move you will have to try and relax just a bit. Even just a bit of teasing is a great way to flirt and this works best with someone you have talked to at least a few times. You don't want to tease someone you have just met because they may think that you are being serious.

You want to get caught looking at the person. You definitely don't want to stare at them, but getting caught glancing at them is great if you want to make sure they know you are interested.

Making eye contact is another easy, but subtle way to flirt. This can be slightly uncomfortable for an introvert but remember you don't have to stare into their eyes just a quick glance, making eye contact when they say something important or when you compliment them.

When you make eye contact, smile at the person. This will let them know that you are interested in them. If the person is across the room then smile slowly.

You should also learn how to use body language. Make sure that you keep your body turned toward the other person and do not cross your arms or legs. Crossing your arms gives the impression that you want to distance yourself from the person and this is not the impression you want to give.

Finally, you are going to have to break the touch barrier. Even if you just slightly brush up against the person, make sure that you touch them. Any form of touch shows that you want to be close to the person and is a great way to flirt.

Flirting is very important if you want to be successful at dating and if you want to leave the other person with a good impression of you. If you go on your first date and do not flirt at all the person is going to think that you are not interested in them. On the other hand, you do not want to overdo it with the flirting because it will only make you look desperate. Balance is the key when it comes to flirting, especially on the first date.

Limiting Beliefs and Dating Falsehoods

In his usual pithy form, Wilde sums up many unhealthy societal views about sex, dating and the entire courtship and mating process. No other topic on this Earth is more consumed by bad ideas, societal brainwashing, and misconceptions. It is also a major source of insecurity and personal self-esteem related problems. How can we tackle so many issues in one chapter? Well, I will certainly try my best. Let's get started.

When Sex and Dating Is About Power versus Love

Perhaps one of the reasons dating and courtship is a topic people find intimidating is because it's interwoven with ideas about self-worth, sexual identity and the power associated with sexual desirability. Other people are more stricken by these thoughts than others, but everyone is affected in some way. This ultimately explains everything from chronic loneliness and the involuntarily celibate, to massive divorce rates.

Covetous, jealousy, manipulation, viewing people as conquests—these are all the vices of the mating game. And, the more that you play in that arena, the more you may find that your love life suffers as a result.

These attitudes are best illustrated in the nightclub or any party centered, social atmosphere filled with strangers. The assumed social roles immediately come to the surface—the women are the targets and the choosers and the men are the seekers. Women cluster together with their drinks, in their respective social circles. Men from the outside stare at them, wondering how the hell they're supposed to go and talk to them.

And soon, men begin trying their best. They memorize openers and routines off the internet, which are generally fake and uninteresting. Many of them have a dual purpose to try and show off to their buddies—after-all, sexual prowess is a symbol of masculinity. One by one, they approach—and get destroyed. The women put up their "disinterested" body language—arms crossed, purses in front of them, and they play the Friday night game of shooting torpedoes at would-be suitors.

After a while, one of the ladies finds herself somewhat attracted to one of the men—maybe it's his dark hair, strong cologne, and excess confidence. And so, she begins entertaining his attention and she leaves her group and goes to the bar with him.

Their conversation is not that interesting—it's about her pet cat. The man nods in feigned interest as he sips his Manhattan and listens to her, but secretly he's wishing he had found one of her friends instead of her. Although they're far from ripping each other's clothes off—on the outside, their uninteresting exchange actually looks like he just pulled her from her friends in a stroke of social brilliance and is now seducing her like a true Don Juan.

What happens next is almost as predictable as clockwork—the other guys in the club start to feel jealous. Because they assume Don Juan is more skilled and with greater sexual prowess than them, they begin harshly criticizing themselves. In the movies, real men go to nightclubs and score one night stands and each guy watching Don in action is forced to think "How am I so inadequate? What is THAT guy doing that I'm not?"

Among the jealousy mongers, one guy, in particular, decides he will NOT be fucked with. Don Juan can go to hell, HE is the true alpha male. And so, he buds into their conversation. He hands

Don his Jagerbomb and inserts himself in-between the two of them. The woman's now feeling a bit warm and fuzzy thanks to her Cosmopolitan and her inhibitions have weakened. And so the alpha male's brute grab for attention is temporarily interesting to her. She entertains his attention long enough to piss Don off, and the squabble that results between Mr. Alpha and Don quickly turns uncomfortable, and she retreats to her friends.

After some harsh words are exchanged, the bouncer detects a fight brewing; and both guys end up kicked out to the curb. The alpha dude dusts himself off, collects his friends and goes to the next club. Don Juan goes home angry and avoids going to the clubs again for a couple of months. The lady in the story returns home to her three pet cats, curious why she has such bad luck.

If that story sounds familiar to you, it's how the mating process seems to inevitably play out again and again. If you read between the lines in that story, you'll notice a lot of twisted dynamics, and in a way, it's everybody's fault for playing into it. The end result is that very often—nobody wins. While I don't doubt that some people do hookup at nightclubs, in real life (not Hollywood), the only thing most people sleep with at the end of a night on the town is their pillows.

The women, in many ways, enjoy the attention. They like to be seen in crowded venues, and while they may complain about "annoying guys", in truth they enjoy the sense of power that comes with rejecting 90% of their potential suitors. It's the same phenomenon as being addicted to posting selfies—it's a high received from sudden self-approval and attention. It is narcissism made manifest and it's not healthy.

As for the men, in most situations, the women become synonymous with sport. Men take their sexual abilities VERY seriously and they continuously judge each other about it. The word "virgin" is used among male circles as the lowest form of insult. And, when you have men's self-esteem and egos on the line, inevitably you get jealousy, anger, pushy behavior and all-out fistfights. And, it's not healthy.

If you think these problems end beyond the bars, you're wrong. The same vices appear again later as men "show off" their girlfriends; getting high from the jealousy others feel. It also manifests when women use sexuality as a method of manipulation; perhaps chatting up an attracted male in front of her partner as a means to spur jealousy and manipulate him into behavior that she desires.

Some would argue the majority of this behavior is biological. Others say it's sociological, related to gender roles. I might say it's about good old-fashioned emotional immaturity. Nonetheless, perhaps now you can see what Oscar Wilde was talking about. The mating game is rarely as simple as meeting someone and enjoying the chemistry. Instead, so often, all of these vices are interwoven into it.

Some Proposed Solutions

The difficulty with being a shy, introverted type is we may be slightly more sensitive to these negative aspects of the mating game. As a result, it's one of the many reasons we may choose to be alone on a Friday night with some wine, a movie and (inevitably) a pet cat or dog on our laps.

The best way to fight against the dark side is to make sure you've eliminated the habits from your own life. Naturally, you'll attract a higher standard of people as a result.

Some of this advice is geared toward men and others toward women—it should be fairly obvious which is which.

Don't Treat Women as Conquests, Yes Even the Pretty Ones

There is a common phenomenon where men like to place women on pedestals; namely for physical appearance factors. I think this condition is exacerbated in the 21st century when youth and beauty are literally worshiped and men are force-fed diets of pornography.

As a man, I find nothing wrong with finding myself stricken by a beautiful woman. In fact, it's an AMAZING feeling—I love it. However, it's NO excuse to prop that person up as something you can show off. This goes back again to that ego-driven lust for power. A man wants to feel powerful, to be able to say he acquired some woman that only exists in every other male's fantasies. There are a lot of obvious reasons this attitude will hurt you—namely, it's reducing human beings to materiality and status.

And, by the way, ladies—you're not exempt from this behavior. I used to go to school with an Abercrombie & Fitch model. Every girl on sorority row wanted him solely for the status that would be associated with dating him. Trust me, he was not as happy about this situation as you may guess. Being reduced to a status symbol is not fun for anybody.

Men Who Approach You Are Not Malicious, They Just Want Hugs

Being a male, I've spent a great deal of time with fellow males and I can say with some degree of certainty that most of the guys I've been out with on weekends who start approaching women are neither rapists nor do they feel entitled. In reality, they're insecure and really want some type of human interaction.

In my story earlier, I used the analogy of women shooting potential suitors down like torpedoes. Sometimes this is necessary when that one pushy, clingy jerk doesn't get the message. However, if you're perpetually single, you may consider letting your defenses down a little bit.

It's easy to get into the habit of constantly rejecting; constantly exerting your power in the sexual marketplace, but again—it won't cure your inability to find a date. Before you judge the guy for being geeky, creepy, douchebaggy, or any other "y" adjective, try talking to him and see if there isn't some type of chemistry. Often we click surprisingly well even with random people.

And, do keep in mind when a guy approaches a girl, he's sometimes mustering as much courage as he possibly can. He may be a fellow shy type who is completely going outside of his comfort zone. That should be admired at least a little bit, right?

Treat Your Sexuality as a Gift, Not a Weapon

I would say this applies to both boys and girls. Don't allow your sexual charisma to go to your head. As soon as attraction, sex and dating become egocentric, you're in trouble.

From the woman who's so striking that every single man stares at her with desire, to the man whose words are so smooth that few women can resist, a few of us do have these charms. Such abilities do not, however, make you more special than anyone else.

The fact that you can create sexual desire means it should be handled cautiously and with respect. If you attempt to use this ability as a means to siphon value and exert power, you could become a force of darkness instead of good.

I've seen it myself in the murky world of pickup artists and professional seducers; allowing their sense of ethics to take a backseat to finding the next conquest. This is where sex once again becomes about power. Interestingly, those guys who are obsessed with obtaining more notches than their peers often share commonalities of not being very happy; and not finding meaningful relationships. Certainly, the same behavior can manifest in women, as well.

If you find you have the ability to turn others on and be sexually appealing; think about how you can use it to make your future partner happy, not about how you can exploit it to seduce and destroy.

People Do Not Represent Their Genders

There is festering hatred in this world and a sizable chunk of it is related to gender animosity. I point the finger directly at vicious genderist movements and websites—including both certain "Men's Rights" communities as well as extreme feminist ideologies.

Genderism exists as a result of a predictable behavior pattern: "a boy or girl hurt me, therefore all boys or girls are this way". Get a bunch of people like that in a room together and they form a club. It's all downhill from there.

Sweeping judgments are easily the lowest form of human consciousness. It spurs everything from racial hatred to religious violence. Never characterize the opposite gender, even in jest. Never say "All men are this way" or "All women are that way".

Doing so places your love life in permanent jeopardy. It may also hurt all future relationships. Logically, there is no excuse for this type of thinking. The action of one person does not and never will reflect some greater trend among people.

All People Are Your Brothers and Sisters

Uh oh, this sounds a little creepy, huh?

Hear me out. Stop sizing people up based on whether you'd date them or not date them. Whether they turn you on or don't turn you on. Or, how badly you want to acquire someone and beat everyone else to be the first to get him or her in the sack.

Competition models of reality are toxic and sizing people up as objects is doubly toxic. Instead, consider that everyone is your brother or sister at their core.

Seek to put people on the same level playing field as you. A supermodel does not have more status than a cashier. A hot billionaire CEO does not have more status than the guy who takes out your garbage. So, don't make dating decisions based solely on societal identified status—because such an ego-driven box will severely limit you and spread unhealthy outlooks of the world.

The Dangers of Needing Validation and Approval

One of the patterns of thinking that endanger your love life the most is seeking validation and acceptance. While this is a systemic problem that takes many forms, it expresses in the dating world as neediness, clinginess and trying to move things forward too fast. An example might be asking someone you've known for two weeks to move in with you. Other examples include any form of stalking or obsession about your partner.

The core of this limiting belief is: "I'm not good enough as I am". If you bring this mentality into dating and relationships, it will cause a lot of problems. For one thing, you'll always be looking for patterns to reinforce this idea. Any type of perceived rejection will be taken to heart and be a confirmation of inadequacy.

Needy, clingy behavior can kill things before they ever start. Somebody who's emotionally sound will sense there's something "off" about you and they will not pursue things any further. This mentality breeds emotional inter-reliant relationships and people who are not codependent will steer clear of you.

During such conditions may be in the realm of psychiatric care. However, you can start by training yourself to be self-accepting. Self-development is truly about letting go of conscious and unconscious negative patterns about yourself. This includes feelings of inadequacy about your physical appearance, speech, social skills, status, worthiness among peers and so forth.

Unfortunately, in schools, emotional intelligence is not taught. How well we accomplish our goals and fulfill our roles in society is of the utmost importance, but how happy and self-accepted we are is not even taken into consideration. It is no wonder that people leave the educational system well-trained in their vocations but emotionally and psychologically vulnerable.

I have no idea how badly affected you might be by these negative ideas, but be mindful about your insecurities. Just remember that the less energy that you give to your perceived flaws, the less power that they have over you.

The Ten Percent Disease

Living in Los Angeles, I've found the "ten percenters" to be very common. This is another odd philosophy that definitely hurts people's love lives.

In the big city, many of us are career-minded. Los Angeles, New York, London—these are places where competition is fierce and the desire to reach the top is strong enough to blind people with ambition. In much the same way that people strive for the best job, the highest salary and the most fame—people also competitively seek the best mates.

In many ways, this doesn't make any sense—how can we compete with getting the best partners? This indicates that people are valued based on a gradient scale that's somehow universal. It neglects the fact that compatibility differs between people. It turns all of our relationships into a status-based pursuit.

The ten percent disease is when a person seeks only what they perceive as the top ten percentile of partners. They will mercilessly weed out candidates who do not fit their standards of being "the best".

These are the ladies who subscribe to the rule of 6's (six pack abs, six figure income and six feet tall) or the men who place great judgments about things like hip ratio, symmetry, boob size, etc.

Their never-ending quest is to find the perfect woman or "Mr. Right". They would rather live alone and never find a partner than settle for somebody who's "second rate". They place their love lives on the same playing field as their careers and quest to reach the top of the social hierarchy.

And, they are reinforced in this behavior by the media, peers, TV shows, etc.

In reality, ten percent syndrome is part of the same insatiable materialism that plagues so many and creates endless unhappiness. Not only does it severely limit your dating pool, but it makes you judge people's worth as human beings on meaningless criteria.

When this syndrome is in action, a man or woman will be perpetually single, as going on dates with such a person will be uncomfortable for the other party, because it will always feel like a job interview is taking place. Instead of relaxing and getting to know such a person, the victims (dates) will instead feel like they are in the hot-seat; with no room for error.

Without fail, when decent people run for the hills around ten-percenters, he or she will rationalize it by saying "Oh, that date wasn't good enough for me anyway". The truth, however, is that their crushingly complex standards are limiting their choices to only a small percentage. If they ever do find someone, it was after basing most of their standards on surface level things ("Wow! He's a TV producer") and then they become disappointed when they find out there was no real connection after all.

And thus, we have massive divorce rates in the United States and many other countries!

Don't be a ten-percenter. It's good to have standards, but there's a difference between having such standards and being a closed-minded pursuer of some pie- in-the-sky perfect mate. Further, if you base your love life as something akin to you professional quest-for-the-best, you will always be sorely disappointed.

Dating Tips for the Introvert

As you can see it is not very difficult to start dating even if you are an introvert. One of the hardest steps that you will have to take when it comes to dating is to actually get to the date. As an introvert it is so tempting to cancel the date with some made up excuse just minutes before it is to take place, but if you can get past that you will have a great time and possibly spend time with someone who will be in your life for the rest of your life.

In this chapter, I want to give a few tips that you can use while you are on your first date. The great thing about these tips is that not only will they get you through the first date, but they will help you on the 5th date, the 10th date, and the 23rd date. Keep these tips nearby for quick reference and you will find a lot of success when it comes to dating.

Be yourself. Don't try to pretend to be some sort of social butterfly when you really are not. If you are feeling uncomfortable in a social setting, simply tell your date. One great thing that you can do if your date asks you where you would like to say go, something like this: "I'm a bit of an introvert so if we went somewhere where there were not a ton of people I'd be a bit more comfortable." This allows your date to understand your personality type and allows you to be honest about how you are feeling.

Avoid dating someone who does not allow you to get a word in the conversation. A relationship is about give and take and when someone will not even let you talk, chances are they are more about taking than giving and are not the type of person you need to be in a relationship with.

Try to find things that you have in common even if they are small and focus on them. Finding things that you have in common is going to help you to build the foundation of your relationship. It does not matter that he likes steak and she likes chicken but if they both love a specific television show at least they will have something to discuss.

Make sure that you wear clothing that you are comfortable in. Yes, this is a dating tip. If you are not comfortable in what you are wearing you are not going to be comfortable on the date and the date is not going to be enjoyable for you. If the date is not enjoyable for you then it will not be enjoyable for the other person either.

Don't worry about getting physical. As an introvert, it is going to take time for you to build that type of bond with a person and if you feel they are pushing you too far too quickly then tell them. If they don't accept what you have to say, end the date and go home, they are not the person for you.

Do not put yourself down while you are on your date. As an introvert, I know it is extremely easy to put yourself down or always apologize just for being yourself. Do not do this. If the person is really interested in you then they will not like the fact that you are always putting yourself down and you don't have to apologize for being exactly what they are interested in.

Don't brag while you are on a date. This can be hard to do if you have had a lot of success in any area of your life. Save the sharing of your success until you are actually in a relationship and your partner can take pleasure in it as well. Otherwise, you may end up making them feel as though they are not good enough for you.

One of the main things that you are going to have to remember when you are going on a date is that you are going to have to talk. No matter where you go or what you are doing on a date you have to talk to the other person. This means that you are not going to be able to be prepared for every question they are going to ask and you are going to have to let go of some of the control.

A few ways that you can prepare yourself for this are: Start practicing talking to strangers. Try chatting with the cashier when you are checking out at the grocery store, talk to your friends online or join an online dating community, or have one of your friends introduce you to their friends.

You can start slow when it comes to interacting with strangers. Smile at people you pass, say thank you and make eye contact with the guy who opens the door for you or opens the door and smile at the cute girl who is walking into the gas station at the same time as you.

When it comes to letting go of control, you may want to consider taking part in an activity where you have very little control over the situation. For me, it was going canoeing with a friend on a very rough river. I had no control of the situation at all and had to learn very quickly to accept that. I also had to learn that by tensing up instead of relaxing I raised our chances of flipping the canoe over. Taking part in an activity like this will help you to learn how to relax and allow whatever situation you are in to take place even if you cannot control it.

It is best if you take part in these types of activities with a close friend that you trust so that you are able to relax a bit instead of completely tensing up like you would if you were with a total stranger.

Another thing that you need to remember is that you don't have to put people on a pedestal. You are every bit as good as they are, no matter how attractive, how successful, how much of an extrovert or how rich they may be. When we put people on a pedestal we are saying that they are better than us and that we do not measure up and although this is something that introverts do all of the time it is not healthy to do this when you are dating. Instead, try to remember that they are human just like you and even though you may not be able to see their flaws they have them.

When you first begin dating I suggest that you try to date someone with a personality type similar to yours. This is not to say that you need to date someone who is an introvert that would be quite a boring and difficult date, but you should also avoid the extreme extroverts as well. Those who prefer to be loud, draw attention to themselves and cannot exist outside of a large crowd are not the type of people you should start off dating.

If down the road you become more comfortable in social situations than you might consider dating these people, but the chances of this happening are very slim.

Making a Great Impression

When you go out on your first date the main thing you are focused on is making a good impression. This is why we spend so much time preparing for the date. If you are a woman you may spend hours getting ready ensuring that your outfit, hair, and nails are perfect. If you are a man you may spend a ton of time ensuring that you have the perfect date planned and that you look your best all so you can leave a great impression on your date but there is more to making a great impression on a first date than looking good.

If you want to make a great first impression you need to have things to talk about. I discussed this a bit when I told you that you need to make sure that you have a life that you enjoy full of things that you enjoy. If you don't have anything to talk about you are not going to be interesting to the person you are going on the date with. You also want to make sure that you have a wide range of topics to talk about in case the person is not interested in certain topics that you enjoy. You should avoid any political talk until you have gotten to know each other better, avoid talking about current events as well because these topics can be filled with emotion and be upsetting for both parties.

While you are on your date, remember that your date is just that, a date. They are not your therapist, your parent or your best friend. Do not ask for advice on issues that you are having in your life, do not complain about how hard your life is at the moment. Instead, stay upbeat and positive. Your goal is to have fun and make sure that your date does as well, not get advice on your life, save that for someone else.

Before ever going on your first date you need to make sure that you are choosing your date by not only using your heart but your brain as well. You may find someone extremely attractive and you may find that you are dating those that you feel sorry for, instead of doing this, have a list of attributes you want your date to have. These should not be physical but should pertain more to their personality. You know what you are attracted to physically but often when we are attracted to a person physically our thought process goes out the window and we end up in bad relationships. If the person does not match what is on your list then no matter how attractive they are you should not date them.

In order to make a great impression when you are on a date, you are going to have to work on your communication skills. Remember when I told you that no matter what you do on your date you are going to have to talk? This is where this comes into play. Practice with a friend or as introverts love to do, spend some time doing research on improving your communication skills. If you do choose to do the research, just make sure you practice your new skill before the date.

You should also make sure that you show that you are interested in what the person is saying to you. You can lean forward to show that you are listening to what they are talking about, but make sure that you do not slouch. If you slouch when you are on your date you will make them feel as if they are boring you so make sure that you maintain good posture.

When the date is over make sure that if you would like to see the person again, you let them know. It is difficult as an introvert to put yourself out there and tell someone that you would like to see them again, but if you don't then you cannot expect them to know it. Another thing that you should do at the end of the date is to offer to pay for at least a portion of the meal. Even if the other party says that they will pay, if you want to make a good impression, offer to pay for the drinks or dessert. This will ensure that the other person does not feel as if they are being used or that you are the type of person who feels entitled to a free meal. You should also say thank you at the end of the date. One of the biggest mistakes that people do when a date is over is not saying thank you. This person took their time and spent it with you, they may have paid for dinner, a movie or some other form of entertainment, the least that you can do is say thank you.

That leads me to ensure that you prepare for rejection. Rejection is something that many introverts fear, but the fact is that it happens. You are not going to click with everyone you go on a date with. Not everyone you like is going to like you back and there are times that you are going to have to reject people as well. You need to be comfortable with rejection and understand that it has nothing to do with who you are but instead, it has to do with two personalities not clicking.

You may find that you go on a date with someone who is not great for you, but would be wonderful for someone that you know. Even though there is nothing wrong with the person you are going to have to reject them and so it will be with those who reject you.

<u>Marriage</u>

Don't you think it is easier to get something than it is to keep something? Here is a great example: a dog. I wanted to rescue a dog and I thought nothing of the time and effort it would take to take care of whatever dog I would get, I just wanted a dog. I went to a shelter and I rescued what is still the greatest dog on the planet (note my bias). I do love my dog, however, it was simple, it was as easy as grabbing a drink from the refrigerator, to pick out and get my dog; keeping him is another story. I didn't think about how much food he would eat, getting him a collar, a leash, registering him with the county, tags, vet bills, taking him outside, training him and so on. Get the picture? The same applies to relationships. It is easier to get the girl than to keep the girl. I have heard the old saying, "Love is all you need", however, it really is not true. Love is a good thing to have in a relationship and it will help when times get tough, yet maintaining a relationship will take time, effort and a great deal of compromise. As introverts, we have strengths that can assist us in maintaining our relationships and also little character nuances that make us slightly more susceptible to getting irritated or being overly sensitive. Let's talk about some really important things for us to think about, as introverts, when it comes to relationship maintenance.

As men, introverted or not, we must keep our word. As introverted men, we are more sensitive and want our partners to do the same, thus we are more likely to do so. Women are super sensitive to what we say and do and we need to make sure we are true to what we say; we need to make sure that more often than not, what we say matches up with what we actually do. How often are men telling their partners that they will be somewhere at a given time, or spend a specific day with them and then backing out at the last moment? Let's let the answer to that one go because it probably cannot be counted. The fact is that women remember and they remember quite well what we tell them we do and what we do NOT do, probably better than what we end up doing. If you are in a relationship with a fellow introvert, she is likely to be far more sensitive to your word-keeping abilities than an extrovert would be, as well, though dating an extrovert is no excuse to not keep your word. Women are definitely a way for you to be reminded of your integrity, potentially on a daily basis, as they are quite good at telling us what we are doing wrong! Do yourself a favor, do what you say you will do when you say you will do it. No one is perfect and no one expects you to be, so when you fail to keep your word, use your ability of self-reflection and self-correction to set things right.

Respect will go a long way in maintaining your relationship. This is most assuredly a two-way street, so you want to be sure to have conversations with your partner about the respect you deserve as well, which may be difficult for you, but it is a necessity for the both of you. Respect encompasses many areas of a relationship, as well, so this does not mean simply respecting her as she is speaking to you, this also means respecting her space, her need for her alone time and also her separateness, her opinions and so on. Anything that you would want to have respect from your end, respect her in the same manner. Mutual respect will go far and she will notice even little acts of kindness and respect, even if it is simply texting and calling her back in a timely manner. These acts of respect show her how important she is to you and show her that you care.

Sometimes it is easy to get lost in work and obligations outside of a relationship. Even with being an introvert and wishing to stay home frequently, we all have to work and sometimes those demands outside of the home can be draining to a relationship for introverts. I know for me, if work is taking a toll on me emotionally, it will take a toll on my relationship, as I will need more time to recharge emotionally and I will want to keep to myself more often. This has an effect on my significant other because I will want to spend less time with her. Unfortunately, this is the opposite of helpful in the maintenance of a relationship, so I have found that no matter what outside obligations are pulling me in different directions, setting aside time for the two of us intentionally has been helpful in my relationship. Though it may sound slightly cheesy or cliché, it is a good idea to get together and agree on a day or evening to have a "date," even if your relationship is committed and established. Try not to get stuck in the rut of being too comfortable in a relationship that you fail to make special time to simply be with one another, as this can strain a relationship unnecessarily.

Women also respond well to you being in tune with her, which can mean and encompass a wide variety of things. Listen to her, pay attention to the smallest of details of her life, her work, her likes, and dislikes. Every once in a while, though not too often, surprise her with a small gift to show her that you pay attention. If you listen and pay attention and you know that her favorite treat is a white chocolate caramel, then during a week that you know has been stressful for her, go to a candy store and buy her some, put them beside her plate at a dinner that you've prepared for her. Little notions like this will go a long way and will be noted in her brain for a long time. Being in tune with her can also mean recognizing her accomplishments and praising her when she has done something well, taking her to celebratory dinners or simply giving her a great massage if she has worked late one day. You're an introvert, you're great with details and those facts should make this one of the easiest parts of maintaining your relationship!

As much as spending quality time with your partner is important, so is making sure that you take care of yourself in your own time. You need time to be able to recharge emotionally, spend time with people in your circle of friends that are not attached to your relationship and simply be yourself. You may love your partner and feel as though she has become your whole world, and this is wonderful, yet you still need to maintain a sense of identity outside of the relationship. If you rely solely on your partner for everything all of the time, this is another way to put undue strain on your relationship. In order to maintain a healthy relationship, especially for an introverted individual, the ability to have an identity separate from your partner is of the utmost importance.

The strengths that you have as an introverted individual will not only help you in the dating world, as in gaining a partner but will also assist you in relationship maintenance. Introverts are world-class listeners, are intuitive individuals and tend to care about and connect deeply with other individuals. These are all assets in maintaining a relationship. The most important piece of all, however, is the last piece of advice that was listed, and that is making sure you can also maintain your sense of self. You were a whole person prior to the onset of your relationship and if anything were to happen to your relationship, you can be a whole person after. I cannot stress this enough. Not only will this help you maintain your relationship, but it will help you maintain you!

As introverted individuals, our connections with others can become so intense that we can end up having a difficult time deciphering where one person ends and the other begins. This is termed "enmeshment" and is something to avoid in a relationship. Our ability to be so deeply intuitive and our desire to be available for others emotionally make us susceptible to enmeshment. Because of this, it is imperative that we learn to set boundaries in our relationships and are able to see that there is an "I" and a "you," and not just an "us." This is a healthy part of building and maintaining relationships with friends, family, as well as significant others.

Introverts have some needs that are specific to their personality that extroverts may not necessarily need in a relationship. Some of these needs may include quiet time after a long day at work, conversations that include depth as opposed to simple small talk, time outside of the relationship to maintain one's identity, and for men, having time in silence and emptiness. Male brains, in general, thrive in emptiness, and the introverted male specifically, needs more time in emptiness and silence than your average male. It is important that your significant other knows

what your needs are and that these boundaries are
not just set, but are clear so that there are no
issues or gray areas surrounding these needs.

Women are, by nature, sensitive creatures,
introverted or not, so attempting to tell your
female partner that you need quiet time when you
get home from work may be a daunting task, as
she may want to throw herself on you, hug you,
and catch you up on how her day went, if she is
home waiting for you. For an introvert, this could
be seriously over-stimulating. It is not that this
show of affection is unwanted, just that it is too
much after a long day and you may need some
time to simply be, in silence, for just a few
minutes. This is something you and your partner
can discuss in order to avoid you being irritated on
a daily basis and your partner having her feelings
hurt often. The key to this conversation is honesty
and your approach will depend on your partner
and only you will know your partner and how she

will best react to a specific approach, but be honest regardless of approach. Maybe just tell her that you definitely want to be caught up on her day, that you desire that initial hug and kiss when you arrive home, but after that, you need about 10 minutes prior to any further discussion. Chances are she'll be just fine with that if you are expressing that you need this time to detox from your work day and that you will follow up with her afterwards. Most likely, she just does not want to be completely blown off and telling her you will come right back to her will be enough to satisfy her need, and get yours met as well.

Knowing that the male brain thrives on emptiness and that the introvert needs more emptiness and silence than is the norm, this is a boundary that you definitely need to set. This should not be a difficult conversation to have, especially if your partner is a fellow introvert. If your partner is an extrovert, it could also be an easy conversation to have. If your partner is a fellow introvert, ask her if you can both set aside a time during the weekend when you both take some quiet, alone time to recharge in silence, when you will not bother the other and then come back to each other at a specified time later to be with each other. If your partner is an extrovert, see if she would want to have a weekend day that she goes out with her girlfriends while you have your silent, empty time to yourself, when you won't be interrupted. Either way, your partner is likely to respond positively to your approach, as she will be getting something for herself out of the time as well.

Again, spending time outside of your relationship is a big deal here. Mark your calendar for a guys' night, have her mark her calendar for a girls' night. No matter what your choices are, or what you decide to do, you must make time outside of your relationship and this is a boundary that needs to be clearly set from the beginning so as to avoid the trap of enmeshment, as has already been stated. I won't overstate the importance, but trust me on this one, it is highly important!

Making sure your needs are getting met is a big deal and sometimes, as introverts, we have a difficult time with this. I'm sure I have said this before, but we tend to assume that our significant other lives inside our head just as much as we do and this is not true. If we are in a relationship with a fellow introvert, the fact is, she is inside HER head as much as we are inside our own heads. We must set the boundary clearly, we have to use our words, as opposed to simply thinking that the other person is going to read our minds and just know what it is that we need, what our boundaries are and what we need our partners to do. This is our responsibility. So, go out there, have that conversation up front, honestly, and gently, and I assure you, you will be rewarded.

Introverts have low social energy reserves and they need to be recharged quite often. Even being in a relationship can drain our social energy and we need to be open and honest with our partners, whether introverted or extroverted, know that we need that time to recharge in order to keep the relationship healthy. Extroverts look to others to recharge, or to maintain their social energy stores, yet we, as introverts, need to be alone, need quiet, in order to recharge. Some things you can do in order to recharge alone are to go for a run, go to the library alone and read, write in your journal, find a nice quiet spot and meditate or go to a park and just sit on a bench for a while. Whatever you choose, time to recharge is a must and your partner needs to be both aware and understanding of your need for this time.

Knowing Yourself

There you have it, right? Your guide to dating for introverts. You now know what an introverted individual is, benefits and disadvantages of dating on both sides of the introversion-extroversion continuum, where to meet someone, where to go on a first date, what the attraction process looks like and what is beyond your control: so we're done here, right? Absolutely not, as we have yet to talk about the most important part of this entire issue: knowing yourself. I can write a guide for you that is step-by-step and 200 pages long and it would mean nothing if you have no concept of your own identity, your values and how you wish to present yourself in the world. Sound familiar? Let's talk about getting to know yourself and maybe how to do so better because if you do not know who you are, you cannot expect someone else to get to know you.

This is definitely an exercise in existentialism and poses questions that are deep in nature and may lead you on a journey to self-discovery; if so, that is great! You may already have the answers to these questions, having already done self-discovery exercises or are just lucky enough to be extraordinarily secure in your identity and value set, which is great too! Either way, I hope that the following topics and questions will help you, not only in your relationships but also in your daily life as well. Even if you are secure in your identity, it never hurts to revisit some of these questions and maybe update your answers and your feelings on certain topics.

There are three important questions that are deep in nature we need to ask ourselves even prior to finding the person we wish to establish a relationship with. One of the questions is actually who we want to be with, yet that is the final question we ask ourselves, as the first two questions need to be asked and the answers solidly established before we even attempt a relationship. What should we ask ourselves? What do we need to know about ourselves before we invite another individual to share a life with us? Let's start with what sounds like a simple question, but when really dissected, is the most difficult: Who am I?

How does one go about answering a question such as this? Who am I? Well, if someone were to ask me this question, I'd have a reflex answer and simply give my name and my job. I'd say my name and say hey, I'm an author, I write. This, however, does not define me and those answers are not truly who I am. If those are the only ways in which I define myself, I am in no way equipped to be in a relationship with another person. If these are my answers, I need to delve deeper into my psyche and figure out what my purpose in life truly is. So what is your purpose? What are you passionate about? What were some of your dreams as a child or even as an adolescent? Think of things that you like to do for fun; even things that you maybe feel you do not have time for anymore. These are all part of who you are and are a good way to sit down and write out lists, to help you figure out bits and pieces you can put together to create your whole self. Set a goal: define my value set and determine long-term desires and goals. This is a good start in determining who you are and who you aspire to be.

These are also good ways to answer the next question, which is: What is my path in life? Who you are is the key to your path in life. If, in finding out who you are, you realize that you are an activist for animals, and are also passionate about writing, your path in life may be, just as an example, to write articles for magazines and newspapers which are topic-based about animals and the rights you feel they should have. Like I said, this is simply an example. Maybe your path is to further your education and get that degree you have put off for years. Whatever your path in life is, you are the only person who can determine the answer to any of these questions and these answers must be solid, intact before you can ask the last question: Who will I take with me?

The last question, well, we've spent a great deal of time covering this one! Hopefully, you have gained some knowledge of yourself and learned a wide variety of skills which will assist you in finding that person you wish to take with you on your path in life, whatever path that may be. Just know if you have learned nothing else, that being an introvert is a special thing and because you are introverted, you have a vast amount of strengths you can use to your advantage. I am confident that your ability to self-reflect will assist you in finding yourself and putting yourself out there!

How to Find a Job through Networking

So what does it mean to network? Networking involves creating a network or group of interconnected relationships. Depending on your goals, these relationships can be useful to you for many reasons. Your network can aid you in finding new clients or new jobs while giving you access to resources and other business opportunities you may not have had otherwise.

In return, you can pass along helpful information, make introductions and help others to build their connections at the same time. People deal with people and networking is all about making connections on an individual level, as an introvert, this is something you can excel at. By creating this network of mutually beneficial relationships, you can tap into new resources of business.

Networking is all about creating a web of contacts that provides a growing supply of fresh business. People use personal and business connections acquired through various sources to expand their impact and get their product or service on customers' minds. Networking is really all about what you choose to make it. Attending events and collecting business cards won't get you anywhere. Neither will spamming the folks whose cards you collected. The most effective approach involves some work. It's about building and maintaining working relationships with people whose business influence you value.

The Impact of Networking

Networking is an essential part of the success of any individual or business. No person or company can survive as an island. You need to link up to other people to draw new business. A chain is one illustration that you can consider. As one link, you will not be able to reach across a chasm to reach someone who is looking for you. As you add more links to your chain, you'll be able to extend your influence to more and more potential clients and opportunities.

Networking is achieved on a small scale through natural word of mouth interactions. Your server at a restaurant may overhear you and a coworker discussing business at lunch, he or she may direct you to the relevant person. Networking can happen at the office, the dinner table, the beauty salon or anywhere. At this level, however, building a client base can take a long time. Your boss and your business demand more immediate growth. This is where purposeful business networking comes into play.

Everyone attempting to create and expand their networks tries to find each other. This can happen through the internet, one on one meetings or large scale events. Everyone involved understands the purpose of the interactions. This transparency leads to a useful chain of contacts established. Networking done properly will be one of your greatest tools for expanding business and connecting with others.

Why Networking is a Must for Introverts

Many introverts avoid networking altogether or limit themselves to internet based operations. This is a big mistake, as networking can make all of the difference in advancing your career. While the idea of networking can be intimidating to introverts, it is important for them to rely on their own strengths to network comfortably and effectively. There are many ways to expand your network, but avoiding networking events may cost you some useful connections.

Alternative methods of networking often involve more personal encounters with potential business contacts. This might include coffee or lunch dates. You can also employ virtual methods to connect with others. Social networks and blogging are useful tools to use. They are most effective, however, when utilized in conjunction with face to face interactions. People remember faces much better than they remember screen names or email addresses. For this reason, it is to your great benefit to learn how to comfortably and effectively attend large networking events.

Be Sensible, Not Sleazy

People tend to think of networking as a selfish act that takes advantage of the position and resources of other businessmen and women. If you focus on relationship building, rather than selling, you'll do much better in your efforts. You want to create and become part of a web of influential contacts, rather than becoming a nuisance to others in your field.

The reputation of networking has been earned through businessmen and women misusing contact information. Business cards are used only as addresses to bombard with advertising. People also tend to assume that networkers are harassing friends, family, and personal acquaintances with sales pitches. There is a reason for this. Networking can be a sleazy operation when performed this way.

Fortunately, modern networking does not need to be sleazy at all. You'll find that if you reach out to others in the field, they will reach back. There is no need or benefit to bothering personal contacts with your business presentation. You also should avoid being too much of a salesman with your business network. When approached the right way, networking can be a logical and legitimate way to increase sales.

Networking is not a parasitic act, but rather a symbiotic one. You are making use of help from other people. At the same time, you should also be providing them with a valuable link to extend their chains of influence.

Those who network the wrong way will become pests, but it's easy and mutually beneficial to take a better approach. The right approach involves meeting on a one on one basis as often as possible to connect with people and exchange information. From there, it's a matter of following up personally with these new contacts and remaining connected with established parts of your web.

Be Smart to Look Smart

Don't worry about looking brilliant or charismatic.
Instead, worry about presenting pertinent
information and asking thought provoking
questions. There is nothing wrong with using a bit
of humor and interest in your presentation, but
keep it relevant. Be researched. Know your
product or service and be thoroughly
knowledgeable concerning the whole industry
surrounding it. You should also research other
professionals with whom you share commonalities
and from whom a connection would be mutually
beneficial. Make a point of interacting with these
people at your events.

Preparation is absolutely essential to doing well at
large networking events. The following tips can
help you to be ready:

-Be informed about current events, as a means to involve yourself into conversations with others.

-Have business cards.

-Dress for success. Attractive people are magnets, so take some time to look your best.

-Don't arrive starving. You're there to network. If you are busy stuffing yourself, you won't have a free hand to shake hands or reach for a business card. You are much less inviting as a person if you look as though you are busy eating.

-Limit your drinking. It is easy to lean on alcohol to ease your nervousness about the event. You'll make horrible impressions and accomplish nothing if you allow alcohol to rule your demeanor and conversation topics.

-Give your attention to anyone who wants it. Don't catch yourself looking over someone's shoulder, simply because he's speaking about something irrelevant to you. You never know who someone else's connections may be.

-As an introvert, the more homework that you do, the more comfortable, you'll feel at the event. You do not need to be the loudest or most popular person there to be effective. Your preparation and knowledge will take you far, without extraversion.

Personal Appearance Counts

While your presentation and personality are the most important aspects of your effectiveness, your looks do make a difference, as well. You don't necessarily need expensive designer clothing. You do need a neat and clean wardrobe. Clothing should be ironed with sharp creases. Hair should be attractive and styled simply. Don't go overboard with products, such as gel and mousse. Ladies should wear at least some makeup. It may be wise to get some tips from a professional if you are unsure of yourself in this area.

Equally important as your clothing, hairstyle, and makeup, is your personal hygiene. Ensure that your fingernails are clean and that you smell fresh. Overpowering perfume or cologne can be off-putting to people, so keep any scent light. You'll be talking to a lot of people, so it is also important to have fresh breath. You might even keep some breath spray in your pocket or purse. Chewing gum is not advised, as it can be rude. Mints or breath spray are better alternatives.

One of the biggest mistakes that introverts make is to avoid attending large networking events. Large group settings and pointless small talk probably make you uncomfortable as an introvert. Thankfully, you don't need to become an extrovert to make the most of the events. You might never be happy in these settings, but you can be at ease and effective with the right strategy.

Shrinking Your Circle

One of the best techniques to use when entering a crowded space is to think about how to shrink your circle. The idea of talking to all of those people might be intimidating, so don't think about it. Zero in on a small group and attempt to find commonality with them. Tell them about your company, but without giving a sales pitch. Telling humorous or thought provoking stories is a more engaging way to get others interested in what you have to say. As you work your way through groups of people, you will find yourself increasingly at ease and less daunted by the scope of the crowd.

Another way to avoid the shock of entering a bustling room full of people is to arrive early. While waiting for things to get rolling, you'll meet a smaller number of people and find more natural conversations. This also means that the crowd will form around you, instead of you facing a room full of already established conversation. You will be part of the group that late arriving introverts will have to approach. Enjoy your position and make the most of it in the early hours of the event.

If you don't arrive as early as you would like, try not to panic. You may find that conversations and connections are already in progress. Walk into the room and take a quick look around the room. You are almost certain to find at least one or two others, who are looking for someone else. If you cannot spot anyone, head for the bar. You are sure to meet a few people while getting a drink. Even if you simply have a glass of water, this can be a way to make some initial connections. At the very least, you'll feel more comfortable doing something. You don't want to stand still looking like a deer in the headlights.

You can also shrink the group size by getting into a line. Whether it is a line for the bathroom or for the bar, lines provide immediate common ground, as you are all waiting for the same thing. Don't harass people in line or subject them to a speech about your business. Instead, take the opportunity to chat. You might even leave business out of it temporarily; remember your goal is to connect on a personal level.

Ultimately, you will want to shrink down to one on one interaction with contacts that will most benefit you. These events are not about collecting the most business cards. "Cardboard connections" don't do you any good. You want others to remember your face and something about you. Find commonality outside of work topics, as well as within them. This will ensure a more lasting impression and make follow up an easier task.

Once you have established this personal connection, you can then progress toward virtual techniques, such as email, blogging, and Facebook. These interactions are often more comfortable for introverts than the superficial, face to face chattering involved in networking events. These events provide the personal foundation, however, for more meaningful communication later.

Overcoming Social Struggles

Social situations, in general, can be unsettling for extreme introverts. Be prepared so that anxiety does not get the best of you. Practice your interactions with a close friend or family member. It may seem juvenile, but you will get honest feedback and some practice for the real thing. Have some topics in your pocket, should you find yourself struggling to converse. Many people have difficulty in these situations. After your preparation, take a deep breath and just jump into it.

As you approach someone at an event, what do you say? Should you memorize a half dozen cheesy opening lines? The best opener that you could possibly use is very easy to remember—"Hi." It really works. Follow it up with an introduction and brief overview of what you do. Before you know it, you'll be conversing with ease. If you meet in line for the bar, it's easy enough to ask what their poison is or make a joke about the water being too strong for you. Keep things natural. Smile and be friendly, as if you really think that you have something in common. After all, you probably do.

If the conversation is stalling before you accomplish anything, you have two options. You can excuse yourself politely and start fresh with someone new or you can jump start things with the following topic generators:

-Ask about their residence. How far did they travel? What kind of weather are they having? This topic can lead to a lot of other tangents that you can then redirect to a more purposeful goal.

-Ask about family. People love to talk about their kids and pets. Dog owners are a great example of this; if you are a dog owner like me, just be careful not to overdo this if the other person doesn't share your love of animals.

-Ask about the event. Find out how many of them they have been to and how they like it. Do they have much success with them?

-Ask something about their work. If you've already discussed it, remember a specific that they told you and ask for further explanation. It'll get you both talking again and it shows them that you pay attention when they speak.

-You can spend hours chatting with someone that you find a lot in common with but remember that you have a purpose. Don't lose sight of your goal, which is to gain numerous useful business contacts. Always direct the conversation to something pertinent. If nothing is surfacing, move on to another possibility.

Body language is another important part of connecting with people. Leaning against the wall with your arms crossed is no way to invite people to talk to you. Instead, your default pose should be open and friendly. Keep your arms down and hands-free at your side. One hand in a pocket is another acceptable position.

Holding a glass of water can help you to maintain friendly body language. The most effective way to make yourself look inviting is to keep a pleasant expression on your face. Smile when you meet people. Keep your shoulders open toward them and make plenty of eye contact.

Utilize Your Strengths

It is important not to try to pass yourself off as an extrovert at networking events. You will only end up uncomfortable, embarrassed and unsuccessful. Don't memorize opening lines or attempt to rely on rehearsed jokes to make good impressions. This is not your strength and others will not find it appealing. Instead, focus on what strengths you do have and use these to your advantage.

If a relevant joke or story comes naturally in the conversation, that's great. It's also a good idea to think of an engaging way to discuss your business rather than a typical sales pitch. Do not attempt to stray far from your comfort zone, however, or you'll appear forced and unnatural.

Don't Force It

This means, don't talk for the sake of talking. You might not be a chatter mouth but you can be a great listener. Be an active listener, showing others that you are paying close attention. You might be stuck conversing with someone who isn't saying anything relevant to your field. Escape as quickly as possible but do so without being rude. If you are enjoying the conversation, be sure to pipe up with useful information. Contribute anything relevant to the conversation but don't try to take the spotlight. It isn't natural for you and others will see this.

Don't push a relationship if one is not occurring naturally. In the course of a conversation, you might find that you are not connecting in a manner that you had hoped. Don't drag out the interaction. Wrap it up politely and allow the other party and yourself to experience the rest of the room.

It is important not to make enemies at these events. Everyone should leave with a positive impression of you. Even if you don't care at all about what someone is talking about, be well-mannered and attentive, as you never know who their connections are. They might be able to help or hurt you more than you think.

You might manage some face to face time with your number one target contact. Even if you have a fantastic one on one connection going, try not to monopolize that person. Stay in it long enough to ensure a lasting impression, then move on politely, with the promise of a quick follow up.

You are not being fair to her/him or the rest of the room to take up so much of that person's time. The last thing that you want to do is leave someone with a sour impression of you because you kept them too long. It is also more beneficial to you to spend time with more of the crowd.

Exchange Info

Don't get so caught up in finding connections to people that you fail to provide information. Business cards are a starting point. Someone might also have a Facebook profile, blog, personal email or another source that may not be listed on a business card. If you can find deeper ways to connect, you establish yourself with more familiarity than those who grab and go with business cards.

If you really hit it off with someone, attempt to secure that additional source of contact. One way to inspire this is to offer something of your own. In front of them, write down your personal email address or a different phone number to let them know that you value them more than the typical people to which you hand your business cards to.

As you collect a business card from them, take a look at it and ask something, such as, "Now, is this the best way to reach you?" After all, you will be on the lookout for ways to assist your new valuable contacts. Make sure that people know that you intend to follow through with them, just as you would like them to do for you. After the event, do just that. Blow them away. You'll quickly make a name for yourself.

Make Time for You

It can be easy to get stressed in the excitement of large networking events. Remember that sleeping is not the only time you should be alone. Make time to be by yourself to recharge your batteries. If you allow yourself to become stressed and anxious, you will not be making a good impression on anyone. It is better to put your best self out there for a few people than to make a less than great impression on everyone.

These events can pack your schedule, but carve out some down time for yourself. It might be dining alone or an hour of peace and quiet in the morning. However you do it, find time to recoup from the commotion and stress involved in this kind of networking. As you become more familiar with this style of networking, you will find yourself increasingly at ease. Until then, however, it's ok to schedule down time to reduce your anxiety.

If you find yourself becoming overwhelmed and dealing with anxiety at the event, feel free to leave. Take a walk or go for a drive. Your health and comfort are important, so take care of yourself. You won't miss out on too much by getting away from the crowd for awhile. Get some fresh air and clear your head. You are sure to return revitalized and ready to impress.

Take it easy on yourself the first few times that you attend these events. If you are an introvert and have never attended one, you may be overcome by it all.

Allow yourself a grace period for the first few networking events that you attend. This might mean setting lower goals for yourself or possibly leaving early. Don't book too many events close together. As you become more comfortable at these functions, raise your expectations.

Give yourself time between these hectic event weekends to get back into your normal routine and recharge your batteries.

For introverts, there really is no better place than home. Spending time enjoying a relaxed schedule is just what you need to revitalize yourself. You will be more effective and happy if you give yourself this important time space to decompress.

-

What Characteristics Do Successful Introverts Have In Common?

It is because of the overlaps that shyness and introversion share with each other that most people confuse one for the other. If you have ever been told that you are shy, take some time off to think if you are scared of being around people or talking. In addition, contemplate on whether you like being alone because you get the time to think about the questions that your own world presents to you and social interactions are just time and energy draining that you become a part of just because you have to.

If you can relate to these sentences, then you are certainly an introvert and no matter what and how much people tell you so, you are not shy. In order to help you gain better insight on who is an introvert and the signs that need to be looked at before tagging one so, this chapter gives an elaborate list of traits that an introvert possesses and that set him or her apart from other personality types.

Small Talk Is Not Your Cup of Tea

Small and shallow talks are not an introvert's ball game. On the contrary, introverts prefer talks that have substance and depth in them. This is aligned with the fact that introverts are deep thinkers and talks about life, theories and big goals stimulate them like nothing else. However, when forced into a small talk, they will certainly keep up with you to make you feel comfortable. Introverts are inherently sensitive, which is what makes them really good listeners. So, mostly, a small talk with an introvert will end up into a deeper and heavier conversation.

Phones Are a Bliss and a Curse

Introverts are not the best people to speak with over a phone call. Meaningless phone calls may divert their mind from the thinking cycle their minds are absorbed in. However, when they are speaking to the people they like to talk to, phone calls may even last a few hours. So, introverts share a love-hate relationship with their phones.

Don't Expect a Text Reply Right Away

Introverts are the last people on this planet to jump on their phone to read the notified message and send a reply back as soon as possible. On the contrary, they like to wait until they have a free mind to read the text and give the undivided attention required before sending a reply.

Crowds Spell Chaos

Introverts hate the crowds. Instead, they prefer taking on the world, one person at a time. A party or a gathering means a lot of stress for these people and they just can't wait to find a lonely corner for themselves in the most happening of parties.

Being Selectively Social

Finding likable people and conversing with them comfortably doesn't come naturally to introverts for the simple reason that being around people and speaking to them doesn't energize them. Therefore, they need to warm up mentally before getting into a conversation. With that said, once an introvert finds a person they want to invest their time and energy on, they will do it with all their heart and soul.

Gatherings Eat Up Their Energy

Being a part of a group trip or a party isn't what introverts completely dislike. They may attend an event once in awhile. However, once it is done and over, it may take them months and weeks altogether to replenish the lost energy.

Observant and Mindful

In accordance with the always-thinking mode of introverts, they are all aware of their surroundings and observe the smallest and minutest of details about the people they are with. Once people start noticing these qualities of an introvert, the comfort levels rise at a staggering rate.

Wisely Choose Partners and Companions

Introverts don't wear their hearts on their sleeves and you have got to be really special to get the key to their heart. Unless they are very sure about you and your place in their lives, they will not let you in. However, once you manage to break the doors open, you can be sure to get unbounded affection and attention. They just fear to get hurt and to guard themselves against any unwanted circumstances, they build walls that you will need to bring down.

Good Thinkers Are Creative

Creativity comes naturally to introverts. Their ability to pay attention to details and observe the smallest of details makes them amazing artists and innovators. They stand a much better chance at thinking out of the box for the sheer time they spend thinking.

Introverts Make Great Listeners

Since introverts take in stuff from the environment and think about it before responding, they tend to be amazing listeners. They listen to people to understand them and their situation instead of just looking for something to say as a reply. This quality also makes them brilliant advisors. The act of listening is also an introvert's way to show that they care for you and have listened and thought about every detail of information you have shared with them. Just as much as they practice this, they expect the same from their partners or audience.

Over-Introspective, By Nature!

Being introspective and analyzing things before taking action is a good quality. However, introverts tend to overdo it beyond any limit. They tend to over analyze situations that don't even need a thought. Some situations don't have a deeper meaning and need to be forgotten with the moment. This understanding and maturity shall require some effort from a true introvert.

Introverts Argue Selectively

If there is one class of people who truly understand the difference between an argument and a discussion, then it is certainly introverts. They will not give you shallow arguments and may not even argue with you until they have thought well about the issue. Once they have given a good thought to the issue concerned, they will put up their points to you and listen to your part of the story before taking a stand.

Misjudged Flirts

Introverts are amazing listeners and excessively understanding of people's emotions and feelings. Interestingly, these qualities are commonly mistaken for flirt. This is funny in view of the fact that introverts have to warm up to the easiest of conversations and unless prepared, they may find it hard to even say hello.

Happy Loners

Introverts enjoy being alone. There are just no two ways about this fact. To add to that, they need to be alone to get back all the energy they have spent talking. Lonely time with their own self re-energizes them and helps them unwind.

Never Bored

While the rest of the world may call them boring and non-connected, introverts enjoy their own company the most, which is exactly why they never get bored. They are self-stimulated and unlike extroverts who require external stimuli, they have it all within them. The dreams and thoughts are too overpowering for them to even look outside.

Can Be Cynical

Introverts restrict their lives and worlds to their own self and getting into their world and creating a place for yourself can be a journey to the highest peak of Everest. Since they observe, notice and think about every little thing that happens to them, they will test you on a lot of grounds before letting you in. However, once you make a place for yourself in their life, it is going to be worth all the effort.

Small Circle, Few Friends!

Like we said, introverts are selectively social and only the people who have taken the time to break their walls down and understand them will find a place in their heart and life. Not many people have the time and patience for this. As a result, introverts have a really small circle of friends, but the ones that are there are there forever.

Fiercely Guarded Personal Space

Introverts guard their personal space like the most secure fort in the world. They *won't* let the wrong people in at any cost for the simple reason the wrong people will bring in wrong thoughts, which will hamper their thinking process and burn them out.

Write More, Talk Less!

Writing down your feeling and thoughts gives you much more time to think and clarify what you mean when you wish to say something. This is perhaps the reason why introverts prefer emails and texts over phone calls.

Highly Productive Individuals

All the time introverts spend thinking, they brainstorm and create outlines for their goals. This makes them good at their work. In fact, most introverts are perfectionists by nature and they tend to spend a lot of their time attempting to do a thing in just the right manner. They will just not settle for anything less than the best.

Best Judges of Human Qualities

Their ability to look through an individual's appearance and talk, deeper into the details of his or her personality help them read the unspoken and untold. Introverts are inevitably readers of nonverbal cues and know what a person isn't telling them. This quality sets them in a pretty good position to give a judgment on a person's character, skills, and personality.

Good Decision-Makers

The masters of thinking always have all the data and information that they require to make a well-informed decision. Therefore, they make much better decisions than the majority.

Lastly, the magnetic attraction that exists in introverts is a result of the cloud of mystery that surrounds them. They can read people, but it is extremely difficult for people on the outside to read them and even get the slightest idea of what is going on in their minds. However, if they trust you, rest assured, you have a loyal friend for life.

<u>Disadvantages of Being an Introvert</u>

At this moment, you would have already been able to identify what type of introvert you are. And if you have, the next thing you need to know is that there are two sides to every coin. From identifying your personality, it is only proper to continue your understanding by introducing the disadvantages of being an introvert as well. Identify which among these weaknesses apply to you and analyze them as early as now. That way, you can develop your own solutions on how to turn these things into strengths.

Overly Self-Centered

Having a full understanding of yourself is actually great. Not every person has that. But spending all your time understanding only yourself and no one else can be dangerous. As an introvert, you have a tendency to become overly self-absorbed. Being confident about yourself and your knowledge, you tend to act based solely on your own interpretation of things. You consider your thoughts as always right because your mind is capable of thoroughly processing each of them.

You firmly believe that you are a competent individual which is actually a healthy way of seeing yourself. However, you tend to hold onto that idea too much. You think you know things well and you can understand your environment more than anybody else can. Once you see incompetence among others, you tend to completely disregard their opinion and make your choices based absolutely on your own judgment.

Yes, you are an introvert. You can grow and learn things alone. But along the process of growing, you tend to lose your vision on how important it is for you to see other people grow as well. You don't get inspired anymore. You see yourself as the best among the rest. And with that, you might miss the true meaning of success in life – being happy.

Missing Opportunities

Sometimes your way of playing safe in games does not do anything good for you. Admit it. It takes you three "what ifs", five "should haves", two thoughts of failure, seven pictures of possible scenarios, one panic attack, 23 consecutive heartbeats and a wish upon a falling star before taking any action. Whether this is an exaggeration or not, the point is, you are too afraid to take risks.

One thing all types of introverts have in common is that they do not rush things. It is like a means of survival for them. Taking things slowly, but surely is nice and all until you find yourself losing all the opportunities because others are already stealing them from you. You know your talents, potential, and capabilities very well but all of these things come to nothing if you are not willing to take the risk of showcasing them. Some people are not sure of themselves but they have the courage to try new things. They usually end up happy either because they made it or because they learned from it. Do not be afraid to try!

Trapped in Imagination

Do you fantasize about getting married to your ultimate crush? Or daydream in class when you find the subject so boring? What about imagining yourself in situations, which are almost impossible to happen, before you sleep? If you do, it is time for you to assess just how much time you spend doing such and start checking on your real-life situation more often.

Given your wisdom and creativity as an introvert, you are most likely to be comfortable with your own thoughts. This trait is mostly found in thinking introverts. You don't just use your brain to answer questions in exams. You use it to create moments in your mind, as well. Moderate daydreaming is normal for any person. It is a temporary escape from reality, especially from the not so favorable situations. But the idea of escaping reality may go beyond just a normal temporary thing for you. Your unexpressed ideas can create a vault of memories which never happened to you in real life. You may lose grip on reality and be trapped in your own imagination.

Remember, your mind may be powerful but you are definitely more powerful than it. Put it under your control and be careful on how you use your thoughts. You certainly do not want your introversion to evolve into a form of mental illness.

Overthinking

If there was ever a competition for overthinking, the top 50 contestants would have been all introverts. Introverts are the best at overthinking. No wonder they are labeled as the most imaginative individuals around. This is because they can imagine even the most unlikely things to happen. There is a healthy amount of being open to thoughts of different possibilities but some introverts tend to overdo it.

You always have time to think because you always provide time for yourself to be alone. The only problem is that there are times when you find your thoughts uncontrollable and it is hard for you to ignore them. You spend some of your nights bombarding yourself with "what ifs" and "should haves". You sometimes over analyze things which makes tasks complicated even when they are not. Most of the introverts experience the same thing and most them have also learned to overcome it through time.

If you are having an unreasonable amount of sleepless nights or you experience getting abnormally anxious for no apparent reason, you should consider consulting a psychologist or a psychiatrist. There are some people, commonly adults, who are prone to this. It is not a matter of being an introvert or extrovert anymore. It is a health issue that can be properly addressed by the help of professionals.

Fear of Being Misunderstood

In a normal day scenario, introverts are often interpreted by people who are not introverts, themselves. As a result, their actions are not well understood or worse, not understood at all. To cope with this, many introverts simply isolate themselves from the majority of people who cannot probably relate to them. They find it easier than actually explaining themselves to people.

If you fall under the anxious or restrained introvert category, you probably feel the unexplainable fear of being misunderstood by society. You cannot easily open up even to people who are close to you. You fear that your thoughts and beliefs might not be socially acceptable or your stand on certain issues may trigger hate and despise towards you. Help yourself by talking to the closest people you have. You don't need to be understood by a lot of people. Just the people who are important to you are enough. If you want to overcome your fears, it will be best if you start with this one.

Not Social Enough

What is "enough" in being social anyway? Is it a minimum of two human interactions a day? Or a rule that an introvert should have at least four friends? Actually, it could mean a lot of things to other people but to introverts, enough is when they start feeling drained after interacting with people.

If you are a social introvert, you spend most of your social interactions with those closest to you. This is normal. If you are a thinking introvert, interacting with seven people at parties is normal. If you are either an anxious or a restrained introvert, you still talk to at least a person a day and that is normal. The idea here is that being social, for an introvert, does not depend on the number of people they interact with. It focuses more on the amount of time they spend with them. You are not supposed to spend the whole week without even talking to one person unless you are in seclusion, which you are probably not.

Not being socially active enough is only disadvantageous because people might misinterpret it. It is not deemed normal especially when the majority of people around you are used to interacting with each other almost all the time. When you are in a workplace, people expect your expressive cooperation. So, for this cause, it is best to try and learn how to be more communicative.

Creating a Wall That Isolates You from People

All the disadvantages mentioned above, when combined, result in the creation of an invisible wall that can eventually isolate you from people. This is a wall that makes it difficult for you to connect to society. Do not, however, blame society for it because the truth is, you subconsciously created that wall, yourself.

You tend to use your harsh experiences in the past to build a stronger version of yourself. You do not express things as much which makes it a little harder for you to let go of emotions. You get disappointed when people do not understand you in the same way you understand them. You sometimes tend to be insecure when others are chosen because they are more active than you. So instead of you, nourishing your sensitivity as a talent to reach out to others, you bury it because you believe it hinders your success.

It would be disappointing to think that your positive traits end up being the same thing responsible for the creation of that wall. However, look at it as the solution to it as well. If you are the one who built it, it just means you're the only one who can destroy it. All introverts have invisible walls to destroy. Those walls, however, vary in strength-- in difficulty when it comes to destroying them. Take things one brick at a time.

Dealing with Introversion

You have learned from the disadvantages of being an introvert, but don't let that discourage you. In fact, see it as a means for you to better yourself. Now that you know what your weaknesses are, you can start turning these things into strengths. It may sound cliché, but you do have power over them. You can change things if you have the will and discipline to do it.

Dealing with your flaws also means overcoming yourself. It requires a lot of motivation and effort to do. The idea is to improve the old you without losing yourself in the process. Even the thought of it can be exhausting but it will surely be worth it. Invest your efforts into these methods of improving yourself and one day, you will be able to do the things you thought you couldn't.

Accept Introversion and All of Its Downsides

First things first, do you accept introversion as your personality? If yes, do you accept all the disadvantages that come with being one? Before you continue, try answering both questions with yes. Repeat it to yourself until you finally believe that you are fully accepting yourself. It's easy to say yes, but to really believe it and love yourself for your weaknesses isn't always as simple. You will need to learn how to accept yourself sooner or later. But accepting yourself because you want to makes a lot more difference than simply accepting things because you know you don't have any other choice. Your mentality towards introversion is important because it affects everything.

There is no such thing as a better personality type. Thinking of how things could have been easier if you were more extroverted does not help. What helps is you, accepting your own personality. Once you begin accepting your personality, you will realize that you are also becoming more open to people's opinion of you. This, however, is not something you can do overnight. It will be a long but a rewarding process. There is nothing more fulfilling than the feeling of being loved and accepted as a flawed individual. Accept yourself and everything else will follow suit.

Be Open to Opportunities

How do you actually do this if you are that typical introvert who is afraid of taking risks? One word – courage. If someone tells you that doing something takes a lot of courage then collect as much courage as you can in order to achieve it.

Placing a healthy amount of pressure on yourself is the best way to instantly acquire enough courage to do something. But if you are not the kind of introvert who works well under pressure, then learn the best ways of motivating yourself. You are good at assessing yourself so why not use it to discover all the things that motivate you. If you cannot push yourself by your inner drive alone, try seeking out for external stimuli. Find an inspiration!

Relationships always require a certain amount of social interaction and opening up to others. It can be scary to make yourself vulnerable and expose your thoughts, your feelings, your fears, or other things to another person you don't fully trust. But that, too, is a risk worth taking (depending on the person you're with of course), and since I have been married for several years myself, and my partner being more of an extrovert, I know that the ups and downs of such a relationship are worth the effort.

If you want to be a performer in a theater but you are afraid of auditioning, take a moment and imagine many of today's most acclaimed performers. How did they become so great? Were they born good at acting? No. They began with the basics; they, too, went through auditions. Some even went through years of acting school just to achieve the status they have today. Remember that everything takes work. You cannot expand your singing vocals if you are too shy to show off your true range. Your dancing teachers wouldn't know how to assess your dancing level if you're too afraid to show what you can do. Do not be afraid of making mistakes because you will make plenty of these if you truly want to become better and grow.

Don't Overthink Things

Turn your "if only" into "at least." Do not tell yourself, "If only I have studied more, I would have had a perfect score on that exam". Instead, say "At least I passed the exam without studying much. I'll try studying more next time!" Again, everything begins with your mentality. Look at the brighter side of things even if the situation you are in right now isn't as favorable. It might not change the past, but it will help you cope with the future better.

Overthinking, as you have learned in the preceding chapter, happens when an introvert is unable to control their thoughts. One of the most basic ways of stopping this is to not force your mind to add more negativity to the situation. This is particularly tricky and might even result to miserable flashbacks. Instead, relax and think of how those bad memories actually helped in shaping who you are now. If you cannot control what fills your thoughts, try controlling how you see these things instead. Turn a negative into a positive.

Nurture the Ways by Which You Express Yourself

If you are not used to speaking as a way of expressing yourself, the good news is, you do have other options for it. Introverts tend to be creative when it comes to expressing themselves. The only downside of this is that people are not always very receptive to these, often thinking of it as strange and misunderstanding the thought behind it. Should this happen, worry not. The important thing here is that you are capable of expressing yourself in a way other than merely speaking.

Many introverts find alternative outlets of expression. Some turn to writing, others would see music as a great opportunity for this. There are those who use physical activity; whether it be in the form of dance or simply walking by themselves. It doesn't matter how matter how simple or complex the activity is. Remember that the idea here is to let go of any emotions, especially bad ones that are lingering inside you. The more you keep these things inside, the worse you'll feel. So find a way to let them go.

Allow Yourself to Be Alone Sometimes

You might get confused with the process of improving yourself and become convinced that you are, somehow, becoming an extrovert. However, do understand that this is not the case;

First, you cannot just transform into an extrovert— even though you feel as if you're acting more like one. Second, keep in mind that your introversion is not a sickness to cure. Third, you are improving your introversion, not changing it. The reason you need to deal with the disadvantages that introversion entails is that you have a potential in you that needs to be discovered. And the only way to discover it is to surpass your own weaknesses.

But if you start feeling exhaustion during any part of this process, give yourself some time to be alone. Allow yourself to postpone things. Never prioritize progress when it comes to this—as it is not worth becoming drained of energy and even happiness in some cases. If something doesn't feel right, pause and rethink. Do not overdo things. When it comes to the things you want to change, believe that you'll achieve these at some point; there's no real rush to it.

Being alone can be liberating, even if it's only for a short time. This way, you can clear your thoughts, talk to yourself, or observe a silent area to align your worries, concerns, creative ideas and passions.

Be More Social

You may think of this as contradictory to the idea of allowing yourself to be alone for some time. However, it is not. Being alone is your way of recharging yourself as an introvert. But being social helps feed your mind, it widens your perspective and you certainly need it from time to time. Remember, that whilst you have to improve your old self, you can do this without losing your personality in the process. In some cases, if an introvert lacks social interaction, this could be attributed to laziness on their part. Maybe they simply aren't in the mood to go out—that being said, try saying YES to your friends more often. Choose the right people to hang out with so you can avoid becoming too exhausted.

Consider this: a lot of introverts who were once a lot more timid have managed to become more socially-inclined. Sure, they still have the basic traits of introversion, but at the same time, they've also overcome any issues they might have when it comes to social interaction. This, of course, doesn't always come easy. It takes a lot to overcome something, especially if it causes them great fear.

Given enough time, however, these introverts have mastered the subtle art of being more open to society without allowing the best things about their introversion fade away. This small change can actually be confusing for some—but believe that just because you're a bit more social, it doesn't mean that you've turned into an extrovert! There's a lot more that separates these two things; it isn't just a matter of becoming more social or outgoing.

<u>Conclusion</u>

I hope this book was able to help you to gain better insights on your personality type and what you can do to make the best of the opportunities you get. No personality type is good or bad and if given the right direction, you are sure to come out as a winner. In fact, contrary to popular belief, introverts have a sharper thinking ability and stand a better chance at becoming successful leaders and decision-makers in view of the fact that they have a sharper ability to notice, observe and process information. If given the right direction and channelized in a proper way to use their potential for their own benefit, the qualities that introverts are born with will prove to be God's blessings for them.

This book is an elaborate guide to introversion and what can be done to ensure that the true abilities of an introvert are used to their true potential, in the right direction. In order to bring practical benefits and manifest the effects of the advice given in this book, be sure to implement the advice provided and practice it on a regular basis for optimal benefit.

Finally, if you enjoyed this book, please take the time to share your thoughts and post a review on Amazon. It would be greatly appreciated!